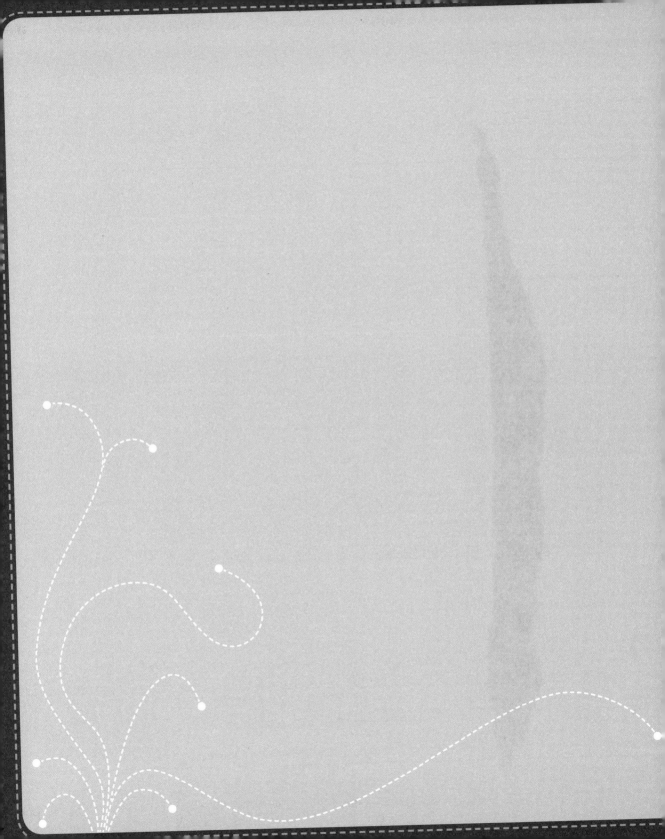

Barack Obama

CHANGE
WE NEED
WWW.BARACKOBAMA.COM

Stephen White-Thomson

W
FRANKLIN WATTS
LONDON•SYDNEY

Franklin Watts
First published in Great Britain in 2019 by The Watts Publishing Group
Copyright © The Watts Publishing Group, 2019

Produced for Franklin Watts by
White-Thomson Publishing Ltd
www.wtpub.co.uk

ISBN (HB): 978 1 4451 6852 4
ISBN (PB): 978 1 4451 6853 1

Credits
Series Editor: Izzi Howell
Book Editor: Stephen White-Thomson
Series Designer: Rocket Design (East Anglia) Ltd
Designer: Clare Nicholas
Literacy Consultant: Kate Ruttle

The publisher would like to thank the following for permission to reproduce their pictures: Alamy: Alpha Historica 10, Everett Historical Collection 18, Newscom 21; Getty: Barcroft Media 8, Laura S.L. Kong 9, Steve Liss 11, Scott Olson 12, Gary Miller 14, Brooks Kraft 15, pyty 6, The White House 19; Shutterstock: Joseph Sohm cover, Action Sport Photography title page, Everett Collection 4, Krista Kennell 5, Michael Urmann 13, XiXiXing 16, Everett Collection 17, Ahmad Faizal Yahya 18, Evan El-Amin 20, Everett Collection 22.

Every attempt has been made to clear copyright. Should there be any inadvertent omission please apply to the publisher for rectification.

Printed in Dubai

Franklin Watts
An imprint of
Hachette Children's Group
Part of The Watts Publishing Group
Carmelite House
50 Victoria Embankment
London EC4Y 0DZ

An Hachette UK Company
www.hachette.co.uk
www.franklinwatts.co.uk

All words in **bold** appear in the glossary on page 23.

Contents

Barack Obama

Barack Obama was the 44th **president** of the **USA**. He was the first black American president.

Obama and his family celebrate after he won the election in 2008.

Barack Obama was president from 2009 to 2017. American people wanted him to make changes to their country.

People chose Obama because they hoped he'd make the USA a better place to live in. ▼

Have you ever wanted to change something?

Early life

Obama was born on 4 August 1961 in Hawaii. Hawaii became part of the USA in 1959.

Where and when were you born?

This map shows the countries that are mentioned in this book. ▼

USA

Hawaii

Iraq
MIDDLE EAST

AFRICA

SOUTH-EAST ASIA

Kenya

Indonesia

Obama's mother, Ann, was a white American. His father, Barack Obama Sr, was a black man from Kenya in Africa. They met and married in Hawaii.

Obama's grandmother lives in Kenya. ▼

Moving around

Obama's parents **divorced** in 1964. Ann and Barack moved to **Indonesia**. Ann married Lolo Soetoro, who was an Indonesian.

Lolo and Ann had a child called Maya. She is Obama's half-sister. ▼

Obama played basketball for Punahou School in Hawaii. ▶

Ann wanted Obama to go to a good school. In 1971, she sent him back to Hawaii to go to Punahou School. He lived with his grandparents.

How do you think Obama felt when he lived so far from his mother?

Learning about life

Obama worked hard at school and college. He learned about **civil rights** leaders who wanted to make things fair between black people and white people.

Obama admired civil rights leader, Martin Luther King Jr. ◀

Martin Luther King Jr.

After leaving college, Obama became a **lawyer** because he wanted to make people's lives better. He decided to work in places where poor black people lived.

Obama trained as a lawyer at Harvard Law School. ▶

Family and politics

In 1992, Obama married a lawyer called Michelle Robinson. They had two children. Malia was born in 1999 and Sasha in 2001.

Obama's family are very important to him. ▼

Sasha

Michelle

Malia

In 2005, Obama became the fifth black American to become a **senator**. He cared for all Americans. He said: "We are one people."

Obama worked in the Senate, which is inside this building in Washington D.C. ▼

Becoming president

In 2007, Obama was chosen to fight the 2008 presidential election. He wanted to make life fairer for all Americans.

▲ Obama's supporters believed he would make good changes to their country.

Obama won the presidential election in November 2008 and became president in January 2009.

Michelle and Barack Obama went to a party on the day that Obama became president.

▼

Do you know who the president or prime minister of your country is?

Being president

As President, Obama tried to change things. **Health care** is expensive in the USA. Obama wanted poor people to be able to **afford** it.

Obamacare helps some people to pay for good health care. ▼

Have you ever had to visit a doctor?

Obama stopped American soldiers from fighting a war in **Iraq**. He worked hard to keep the American **economy** strong through difficult times.

Obama travelled around the world in an aeroplane called Airforce 1. ▶

Re-elected president

In 2012, Obama was elected for another four years as president.

◀ Obama posted this photo on Twitter of him hugging Michelle.

This photo was taken of Obama and his family after his victory in the election. ▶

While he was president,
Obama lived with his family
in the White House in
Washington D.C.
It had been built
by black **slaves**.

**Obama relaxes in the garden of the
White House with his dog, Bo.** ▲

19

Handing over

In the presidential election in November 2016, Obama supported Hilary Clinton. She lost. Donald Trump won.

▲ If she had won the election, Clinton would have been the first woman to become president.

Donald Trump

Trump has very different ideas to Obama of what is best for American people. Obama is no longer president, but he continues to work to make the world a fairer place.

Quiz

Test how much you remember.

Check your answers on page 24.

1 Where was Obama born?

2 Which country was his father from?

3 What is the name of the building where Obama lived when he was president?

4 What are the names of Obama's two daughters?

5 For how many years was Obama president?

6 Who became president after Obama?

Glossary

afford – if you can afford something, you have enough money to pay for it

civil rights – the things that you can do or have, according to the laws of your country. Civil rights often refers to the rights of black people

divorced – when two people have divorced, they have ended their marriage

economy – how money is made and used in a country

election – when people vote in an election, they choose someone they would like to win

health care – the plans a government has to look after the health of the people in its country

Indonesia – a country in South-east Asia (see map on p. 6)

Iraq – a country in the Middle East where American soldiers fought a war (see map on p. 6)

lawyer - a person who has studied the law and who talks for people in a court of law

Obamacare – the name given to Obama's health care plans

president – the leader of a country's government

senator – one of a group of people who helps make laws and decisions

slave – someone who is owned by someone else and has to work for them

Twitter – a website where you can publish short messages

USA – United States of America

Index

Answers:

1: Hawaii; 2: Kenya; 3: The White House; 4: Malia and Sasha; 5: Eight years; 6: Donald Trump

Teaching notes:

Children who are reading Book Band Gold or above should be able to enjoy this book with some independence. Other children will need more support.

Before you share the book:

- What do the children already know about Barack Obama?

- Introduce the idea of the US president as the person in charge of the decisions made by the America government. America is a big and powerful country, so why is it important that they have a good president?

While you share the book:

- Help children to read some of the more unfamiliar words.

- Talk about the questions. Encourage children to make links between their own experiences and the events described.

- Talk about the pictures. How can you tell that some of the pictures were taken a long time ago?

After you have shared the book:

- Why do you think the American people voted for Obama to become their president?

- What do you think were the most important changes Obama made?

- Ask children why they think people in the future will remember President Obama.

- Work through the free activity sheets at www.hachetteschools.co.uk